C000056405

1 MONTH OF
FREE
READING

at

www.ForgottenBooks.com

By purchasing this book you are eligible for one month membership to ForgottenBooks.com, giving you unlimited access to our entire collection of over 1,000,000 titles via our web site and mobile apps.

To claim your free month visit:

www.forgottenbooks.com/free734555

ISBN 978-0-483-78881-7
PIBN 10734555

This book is a reproduction of an important historical work. Forgotten Books uses
state-of-the-art technology to digitally reconstruct the work, preserving the original format
whilst repairing imperfections present in the aged copy. In rare cases, an imperfection in
the original, such as a blemish or missing page, may be replicated in our edition. We do,
however, repair the vast majority of imperfections successfully; any imperfections that
remain are intentionally left to preserve the state of such historical works.

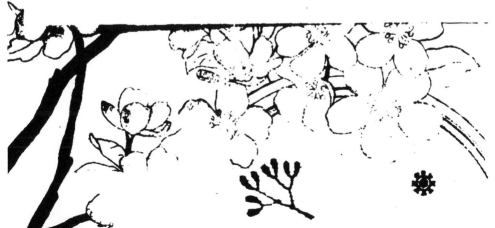

WILLIAM E. *went* GLADSTO

Born, 1809   Died, 1898

RILLIAN
Selected fr
the Writing
WM.
GLA
STON

By F. M. C.

BRILLIANTS

FROM

GLADSTONE.

THE discharge of the daily duties of our position *must* (more or less perfectly) be adapted beyond question either to the supposition that we have a Creator and a Redeemer, or to the supposition that we have not. There is no intermediate verdict of "not proven," which leaves the question open; the question to us is, Is there such proof as to demand obedience? and there are no possible replies in act, whatever there may be in word, except aye and no. The lines of conduct are but two; and our liberty is limited to the choice between them.

When St. Peter, after the prophecy of his own martyrdom, asked our Lord, with a natural curiosity, what should happen to St. John, our Lord replied, " If I will that he tarry till I come, what is that to thee? Follow thou me." So let us not be inquisitive or solicitous to know the judgment to be pronounced upon our brethren, or to solve the enigmas of their destiny, but take heed to our own ; and take particular heed that we do it no prejudice by proud or harsh feelings entertained towards them.

* * *

Virtue, to be truly loved, must be loved for its own sake, not for the hope of reward. * * *

Rapidity of movement was no part of the providential design. Like the seed to which Christ Himself compares the gospel, all the early stages of its life were to be silent and to be slow. Gradually to lay a broad basis of such evidence as ought through all time to satisfy the reason and the heart of mankind, seems to have been the object with which our Saviour wrought.

* * *

During our Lord's life, the bulwarks of the kingdom of evil were being smitten again and again by constant exhibitions of His command over the seen and unseen worlds; and its foundations were being sapped by the winning force of His benevolence and love. . . . When He had died. and risen, and ascended, then the undermining process was complete.

* * *

It appears as if our Lord commonly was employed in those kinds of words and deeds which, repeated in substance over and over again in a large number of places, and before great multitudes of witnesses, were to constitute the main ground of His appeal to the conscience of the world, and the first basis of the general belief in Him.

The Christian thought, the Christian tradition, the Christian society, are the great, the imperial thought, the tradition, and society of this earth. It is from Christendom outwards that power and influence radiate, not towards it and into it that they flow.

* * *

Many are the tricks of speech; and it has become almost a commonplace of our time to set up, in matters of opinion, an opposition between authority and truth, and to treat them as excluding one another. It would be about as reasonable to set up an opposition between butcher's meat and food.

* * *

Christian morals as a whole — as an entire system covering the whole life, nature, and experience of man — stand broadly distinguished by their rich, complete, and searching character from other forms of moral teaching now extant in the world.

WM. E. GLADSTONE.

It constantly excites the surprise of for-
eigners that, when Revolution shakes or
saps the Continent, Authority sits undis-
turbed in England. But that, it will be
said, is temporal authority. It is not temporal authority alone. Rely upon it, the
acknowledgment of a law external to ourselves in things unseen is the absolute
condition under which alone authority can
uphold itself in the sphere of the visible
and tangible.   *   *   *

Every real and searching effort at self-
improvement is of itself a lesson of profound
humility. For we cannot move a step without learning and feeling the waywardness,
the weakness, the vacillation of our move-
ments, or without desiring to be set up upon
the Rock that is higher than ourselves.

*   *   *

We should remember that our religion
itself did not take its earlier root or find
its primitive home in the minds of kings,

philosophers, and statesmen. Not many rich, not many noble were called. The wisdom and the culture were mostly plotting against our Lord, while the common people heard him gladly. The regenerating forces of the gospel made their way from the base to the summit of society; and the highest thought and intellect of man, won with time to the noble service. hired, as it were, at the sixth, ninth, and eleventh hours, wrought hard. and with effect, to develop, defend, and consolidate the truth.

It may well fortify our hold on divine truth, when we observe the desolating and exhausting power with which unbelief lays waste the mind of its victim, and the utter shipwreck that it made of happiness along with faith.

Let us . . . check that impatience of the understanding which so often leads us into

premature and incompetent conclusions upon the personal merits of our fellow-creatures.

* * *

Our life may be food to us, or may, if we will have it so, be poison; but one or the other it must be. So surely as the day and the night alternately follow one another, does every day when it yields to darkness, and every night when it passes into dawn, bear with it its own tale of the results which it has silently wrought upon each of us for evil or for good. The day of diligence, duty, and devotion leaves us richer than it found us; richer, sometimes, and even commonly, in our circumstances; richer always in ourselves. But the day of aimless lethargy, the day of passionate and rebellious disorder, or of a merely selfish and perverse activity, as surely leaves us poorer at its close than we were at its beginning.

* * *

However true it may be that all alike

have sinned, it is far from true that all have sinned alike. There are persons, though they may be rare and highly exceptional, in whom the atmosphere of purity has not been dimmed, the forces of temptation are comparatively weak, and at the same time the sense of duty is vigorous and lively.

* * *

The religion of Christ had to adapt itself to the least as well as to the largest forms of our life and nature, while its central idea was in very truth of such a largeness, in comparison to all we are or can be, as to make the absolute distance between the greatest of human greatness and the smallest of human littleness sink into insignificance. * * *

No more in the inner than in the outer sphere did Christ come among us as a conqueror, making his appeal to force. We were neither to be consumed by the heat of the Divine presence, nor were we to be dazzled by its brightness. God was not in the storm, nor in the fire, nor in the flood, but He was in the still, small voice . . . it was to enter into us, to become part of us, and to become that part which should rule the rest.

CHRISTIANITY IS CHRIST.

THIS was the crown of our Lord's humility, that He was content in this lowly wise to solicit, through the assent of our understanding, the allegiance which he was entitled, as Creator and Master, to command at once from our will.

* * *

On the evil spirits who " believed and trembled," we are told that He laid an injunction that they should not bear witness to Him. Even the proclamation of the truth was not to proceed from the tainted source of a rebellious will and intelligence.

Principles are, indeed, the fathers of opinions. . . . Men, individually and in series, commonly know their own opinions, but are often ignorant of their own principles. Yet in the long run it is the principles that govern; and the opinions must go to the wall. . . . And again. As men may hold different opinions under the shelter of the same principle, so they may have the same opinions while they are governed by principles distinct or opposite.

* * *

It must be recollected that the moral standard of individuals is fixed not alone, and sometimes not principally, by their personal convictions, but by the principles, the traditions, and the habits of the society in which they live, and below which it is a point of honor, as well as of duty, not to sink. A religious system is only then truly tested when it is set to reform and to train, on a territory of its own, great masses of mankind.

WM. E. GLADSTONE.

A scheme came eighteen hundred years ago into the world . . . which has banished from the earth, or frightened into the darkness, many of the foulest monsters that laid waste humanity; which has restored woman to her place in the natural order; which has set up the law of right against the rule of force; which has proclaimed, and in many great particulars enforced, the canon of mutual love; which has opened from within sources of strength for poverty and weakness, and put a bit in the mouth, and a bridle on the neck, of pride.

* *

In beseeching especially the young to study the application to their daily life of that principle of order which both engenders diligence and strength of will, and likewise so greatly multiplies their power. I am well assured that they will find this to be not only an intellectual but a moral exercise.

A life that is to be active . . . ought to find refreshment even in the midst of labors; nay, to draw refreshment from them. But this it cannot do, unless the man can take up the varied employments of the world with something of a childlike freshness. Few are they who carry on with them that childlike freshness of the earliest years into after-life.

* *

Nor let it be thought that those who are never called to suffer in respect to bodily wants, therefore do not suffer sharply. Whereas, on the contrary, it is well established, not only that though the form of sorrow may be changed with a change in the sphere of life, the essence and power of it remain, but also that, as that sphere enlarges, the capacity of suffering deepens along with it, no less than the opportunities of enjoyment are multiplied.

It must be borne in mind that our intellectual as well as our moral nature is ever liable to be powerfully affected by habits previously formed. We know, for instance, that a statesman, a divine, and a lawyer, each fairly representing his class, will usually take different views of a subject, even where they agree in their conclusions, because they approach it with distinct predispositions. These predispositions are the result of their several employments, which propose to them the several ends of policy, law, and divine truth, and modify their common mental acts accordingly.

*   *   *

Philosophizing upon human action, we must collect its laws from a legitimate induction; and we cordially subscribe to the principle that "God, who has given certain laws to our souls, could not make it a moral duty for man to act against them."

It is not the greatness or minuteness of the proposition, but the balance between likelihood and unlikelihood, which we have to regard whenever we are called to determine upon assent or rejection. It is true, indeed, that when the matter is very small, the evil of acting against probability will be small also. But this shows that, in a practical view, the obligation of the law becomes not less, but more stringent, as the rank of the subject in question rises; because the best and most rational method of avoiding a very great evil, or of realizing a very great good, has a higher degree of claim upon our consideration and acceptance, in proportion to the degree of greatness belonging to the object in view.

* * *

The very same principles which govern action in common life, cognizable with common-sense, are those which, fortified (we should hold) through God's mercy with a

24

singular accumulation and diversity of evidence, demand reception of the word and implicit obedience to it ; . . . we cannot refuse this demand upon the plea that the evidence is only probable, and not demonstrative, without rebellion against the fundamental laws of our earthly state.

* * *

To testify to a positive truth, to a living principle, is not only a duty, but . . . animating and ennobling.

* * *

Genius, unless guided by a malignant spirit, has an indefeasible claim to our sympathy in its reverses, and in its achievements to our fervid admiration ; nor is there any more touching, any more instructive, lesson, than such as are afforded by its failures in the attempt to realize, out of its own resources, and without the aid of Divine revelation, either intellectual contentment or a happy life.

It is a cardinal truth that no study whatever can be dry . . . to a mind when earnestly embracing it.

* * *

The highest functions of the human being stand in such intimate relations to one another, that the patent want of any one of them will commonly prevent the attainment of perfection in any other.

* * *

The highest poet must be a philosopher, accomplished like Dante, or intuitive like Shakespeare. But neither the one nor the other can now exist in separation from that conception of the relations between God and man, that new standard and pattern of humanity, which Christianity has supplied.

* * *

There can be no more futile, no more mischievous, conception than that faith is to be kept entire by hiding from view the melancholy phenomena of unbelief.

WM. E. GLADSTONE.

Never let it be forgotten that there is scarcely a single moral action of a single man of which other men can have such a knowledge, in its ultimate grounds, its surrounding incidents, and the real determining causes of its merits. as to warrant their pronouncing a conclusive judgment upon it.

*   *   *

Prove all things. hold fast that which is good. is a precept which England has fearlessly accepted, and from the universal application of which she has not shrunk. . . . It is, we believe. to this cause that we may refer the unquestionable fact that classical studies in this country are not found to have any sceptical tendency. . . . But then there must be real and vital activity of the mind upon the subject-matter of religion, as there is upon the subject-matter of pagan learning. . . . We should begin to shudder for the consequences, if our Christian studies were to become shackled, dry, and formal.

With a sigh for what we have not, we must be thankful for what we have, and leave to One wiser than ourselves the deeper problems of the human soul and of its discipline.

* * *

It is common to misunderstand the acts of an adversary.

* * *

The truth is that —— was not only accustomed, like many more of us, to go out hobby-riding, but, from the portentous vigor of the animal he mounted, was liable, more than most of us, to be run away with.

* * *

Sad as it may seem, the heroes of the pen are in the main but as " fools," lighted by the passing day on the road to dusty death.

* * *

Posterity will have to smelt largely the product of the mines of modern literature;

and will too often find the reward in less than due proportion to the task.

* * *

It is upon the surface that an ordinary life is passed, and that its imagery is found.

* * *

For works of the mind really great there is no old age, no decrepitude. It is inconceivable that a time should come when Homer, Dante, Shakespeare, shall not ring in the ears of civilized man.

* * *

None of his experience passed by him idly, like the wind; all had fruit for him; all left a mark upon his mind and character.

* * *

But the business of a sermon is to move as well as teach; and if he teaches only without moving, may it not almost be said that he sows by the wayside?

Our Saviour is not a mere man, but is God made man; He ought not to be exhibited in any Christian work as a man only, but as God and man.

* * *

But the student of ecclesiastical history, or even the mere cursory inspector of the records of a few of the councils of the fourth century, knows that it was not until after many a fearful, and even what, to human eyes, might seem many a giddy reel, that a nearly unanimous Christendom settled down upon a centre of gravity, in doctrinal expression, which has been perfectly stable through all the vicissitudes of fifteen hundred years.

* * *

The teaching of half-truths is, indeed, indefensible and mischievous, when they are taught as whole truths. But there is an order and succession in the process of instruction; and that which is not good as a

resting-place may be excellent and most necessary as a stage in an onward journey.

* * *

True faith does not imply the exclusion of all doubt whatever. . . . Bishop Pearson defines Christian belief to be an assent to that which is credible as credible. But clearly, much that is on the whole credible is open to a degree of doubt, although it could not be credible unless the doubt were outweighed, upon a comparison, by the evidences in its favor. What, again, is the meaning of " Lord, I believe ; help thou mine unbelief "? There is in such a case a conflict within the mind; it is divided, though unequally divided. This however, is the exception, not the rule.

* * *

In general we do not imagine that even the nascent belief of Christians is seriously troubled with substantive doubts ; but it clearly has not, and cannot have, nor have the great majority of our rational acts in common life, a foundation in that philosophical completeness of conviction which is *de jure* an essential condition of permanent and absolute freedom from doubt. But, in point of fact, the formation of this mature belief, the mode of dealing with temptation when it arises in the form of doubt, is a higher portion of the discipline of the soul; all that we need here lay down is this: To hold that an absolute intellectual certainty belongs of necessity to the reception of Christianity is a proposition altogether erroneous.

* * *

Christianity does not require the highest degree of intellectual certainty in order to be honestly and obediently received.

* * *

Truth in intention shall be a guide to truth in knowledge.

32

WM. E. GLADSTONE.

The God of Revelation is also the God
of Reason; the laws of prudence and common-sense are laws of religion as well as
life.

* * *

Strength of love, depth or grief, aching
sense of loss, have driven him forth, as it
were, on a quest of consolation, and he asks
it of nature, thought, religion, in a hundred
forms which a rich and varied imagination
continually suggests, but all of them con-
nected by one central point, the recollection
of the dead.

* * *

It is indeed true that peace has its moral
perils and temptations for degenerate man,
as has every other blessing, without exception, that he can receive from the hand of
God. It is, moreover, not less true that,
amidst the clash of arms, the noblest forms
of character may be reared, and the highest
acts of duty done.

The life of our Saviour, in its external aspect, was that of a teacher. It was, in principle, a model for all; but it left space and scope for adaptations to lay the life of Christians in general, such as those by whom the every-day business of the world is to be carried on.

* * *

I know not whether there is any one among the many species of human aberration that renders a man so entirely callous as the lust of gain in its extreme degrees. That passion, where it has full dominion, excludes every other. It shuts cut even what might be called redeeming infirmities.

* * *

Beauty is not an accident of things; it pertains to their essence; it pervades the wide range of creation: and, wherever it is impaired or banished, we have in this fact the proof of the moral disorder which disturbs the world. Reject, therefore, the false philosophy of those who will ask what does it matter, provided a thing be useful, whether it be beautiful or not; and say in reply that we will take one lesson from Almighty God, who in His works hath shown us, and in His word also has told us, that " He hath made everything," not one thing or another thing, but everything " beautiful in His time."

* * *

What we are bound to is this: To take care that everything we produce shall, in its kind and class, be as good as we can make it. . . . It is this perpetual striving after excellence on the one hand, or the want of such effort on the other, which, more than the original difference of gifts (certain and great as that difference may be), contributes to bring about the differences we observe in the works and characters of men.

* * *

It is the wisdom of man universally to

watch against his besetting errors, and to strengthen himself in his weakest points.

* * *

The most disputable of the negatives we have pronounced is that which relates to vanity; . . . often lodged by the side of high and strict virtue; often allied with an amiable and playful innocence, — a token of imperfection, a deduction from greatness. and no more.

WM. E. GLADSTONE.

No doubt conscience is supreme in all matters of moral conduct, including the search for truth. But this does not exclude argument and the legitimate use of the understanding upon questions of conduct; and it is no sufficient answer to reasoning drawn from Scripture, reason, or authority, on a question of conduct, to say, " My conscience teaches me so, and there is an end of it." We must submit to have matters of conscience handled by reasoning or authority; and though we are to protest against sentences of the understanding on matters beyond its province, as, for example, upon absolute dogma, yet even there we must not decline to allow the examination of secondary proofs. Conscience may be the ultimate judge of argument, but this affords no plea for declining to hear it; and to admit such a plea is not to honor conscience, but to allow fancy, humor, obstinate, licentious will, and Satanic temptations to enthrone themselves in its place.

It is devoutly to be hoped that the Church, while she must ask for all that is needful for the vindication of her faith, and must support the petition by the tender, if necessary, of all her worldly goods as a price for that pearl for which she is but the setting, should demand no more ; and should rule upon the side of peace, obedience, and acquiescence, every doubt that does not reach to the very charter of her being.

* * *

We cannot draw the curtain upon the sad picture of Christian division and dissension, without beseeching the reader to offer up to God the fervent prayer, that the afflicting contemplation of such a scene may inspire him with the resolution to " seek peace and ensue it " in the vineyard of the Lord on earth ; and, if he cannot here enjoy his soul's desire, then, that he may be moved by the prevailing discord the more manfully to press towards the mark for the prize of entering

into that rest wherein the unclouded presence of God shall enlighten His people, and
His unity shall infold them forevermore.

*   *   *

It is a blessed thing to think that behind
the blurred aspect of that cause, which we
see as in a glass darkly, there is the eye of
One to whom all is light, and who subdues
to His own high and comprehensive, and
perha s for that reason remote, purposes
all the partial and transitory phenomena
with which we are so sorely perplexed.   It
is not then to be the most boastful or
the most aggressive among them that
will be found to be the least refracted
from the lines of the perfect truth.   It
will be the one which shall best have per
formed the work of love, and shall have
effected the largest diminution in the mass
of sin and sorrow that deface a world,
which came so fair from the hand of its
Maker.

"Act upon Christian principle, and you will come to believe it: act upon what is true in itself, and it will come to be also apparent or true to you."

* * *

In the simple act of taking food, the religious sense has a place. The maintenance of life, though it is a necessity, is also a duty and a blessing.

* * *

All men, though in various degrees, require to be supplied with certain practical judgments. For there is no breathing man to whom the alternatives of right and wrong are not continually present. To one they are less, perhaps infinitely less, complicated than to another; but they pervade the whole tissue of every human life.

* * *

The doctrine that we are bound by the laws of our nature to follow probable truth,

rests upon the most secure of all grounds for practical purposes, if, indeed, the consent which accepts it is in fact so widely spread in the usual doings of mankind, that it may well be termed universal.

For there is no one faculty of any living man of which, speaking in the sense of pure and rigid abstraction, we are entitled to say that it is infallible in any one of its acts.

*   *   *

We find by reflection that no one of our convictions or perceptions can in strictness be declared to possess the character of scientific knowledge.

*   *   *

Belief is bounded, so to speak, by knowledge on the one hand, where it becomes not only plenary, so as to exclude doubt, but absolute and self-dependent, so as not to rest upon any support extrinsic to the subject. It is similarly bounded on the other side by mere opinion, where the matter is very disputable, the presumptions faint and few, or the impressions received by a slight process and (as it were) at haphazard, without an examination proportioned to the nature of the object and of the faculties concerned.

* * *

Everywhere, before us and behind us and around us and above and beneath, we shall find the Power which —

> " Lives through all life, extends through all extent,
> Spreads undivided, operates unspent."

* * *

And, together with the Power, we shall find the goodness and the wisdom, of which that sublime Power is but a minister. Nor can that wisdom and that goodness anywhere shine forth with purer splendor than when the Divine forethought, working from afar, in many places and through many generations, so adjusts beforehand the acts and the affairs of men, as to let them all converge upon a single point; namely, upon that

redemption of the world, by God made Man, in which all the rays of His glory are concentrated, and from which they pour forth a flood of healing light, even over the darkest and saddest places of creation.

* * *

Now, if we survey with care and candor the present wealth of the world, — I mean its wealth intellectual, moral, and spiritual, — we find that Christianity has not only contributed to the patrimony of man its brightest and most precious jewels, but has likewise been what our Saviour pronounced it, the salt or preserving principle of all the residue, and has maintained its health, so far as it has been maintained at all, against corrupting agencies.

* * *

A system of religion, however absolutely perfect for its purpose, however divine in its conception and expression, yet of necessity becomes human, too, from the first moment

of its contact with humanity ; from the very
time, that is to say, when it begins to do its
proper work by laying hold upon the hearts
and minds of men, mingling, as the leaven
in the dough, with all that they contain, and
unfolding and applying itself in the life and
conduct of the individual, and in the laws,
institutions, and usage of society.

*   *   *

Divine truth, as it is contained in the gospel, is addressed to the wants and uses of a
nature not simple but manifold ; and is manifold itself. Though dependent upon one
principle, it consists of many parts ; and in
order to preserve reciprocally the due place
and balance of those parts, means that we
call human are available, as well as means
more obviously divine ; and secular forms
and social influences, all adjusted by one
and the same Governor of the world, are
made to serve the purposes that have their
highest expression in the Kingdom of Grace.

WM. E. GLADSTONE.

All among us who are called in any manner to move in the world of thought, may well ask, Who is sufficient for these things? Who can with just and firm hand sever the transitory from the durable, and the accidental from the essential, in old opinions? Who can combine, in the measures which reason would prescribe, reverence and gratitude to the past with a sense of the new claims, new means, new duties, of the present? Who can be stout and earnest to do battle for the truth, and yet hold sacred, as he ought, the freedom of inquiry, and cherish. as he ought, a chivalry of controversy like the ancient chivalry of arms?

* * *

The duties of Christian and citizen now, as ever, coincide. The religious peace which the latter must desire can only be had by the maintenance of the religious freedom which nothing should induce us to compromise.

BRILLIANTS FROM

The way to conquer men's prejudices is to appeal freely to their good sense, and allow some reasonable scope to their free will and choice.

* * *

Some men, indeed, there are, in all times, who are always waiting for a proper time that never comes — men who either beguile themselves with the idea that they have manhood and resolution equal to acting in great crises, when they have none, or who at best wait upon the chapter of accidents, and find their subsistence in the hope of crumbs which now and then may fall from fortune's table.

* *

The freedom we claim is meant to be a real freedom, and the restraints we would impose upon it are only the inward self-chosen restraints of a filial and reverential spirit.

46

Lightning Source UK Ltd.
Milton Keynes UK
UKHW020239101118
332088UK00006B/70/P